Superfood Soups: Fast and Broth Recipes for Natural Weight Loss and Detox

by Alissa Noel Grey Text copyright(c)2017 Alissa Noel Grey
All Rights Reserved

Table of Contents

Superfood Soups To Boost Your Health..................7

Creamy Chicken Soup..................8

Thai Chicken and Mushroom Soup..................10

Broccoli and Chicken Soup..................12

Warm Chicken and Avocado Soup..................12

Moroccan Chicken Soup..................15

Spicy Chicken Quinoa Soup..................17

Greek Lemon Chicken Soup..................19

Healthy Chicken and Oats Soup..................21

Bean, Chicken and Bacon Soup..................23

Asparagus and Chicken Soup..................25

Italian Beef and Vegetable Soup..................26

Mediterranean Fish and Quinoa Soup..................28

Split Pea Soup with Ham and Barley..................28

Alkalising Green Soup..................32

Superfood Kale Soup..34

Cheesy Cauliflower Soup..36

Slow Cooked Superfood Soup..38

Turnip and Potato Soup..39

Spicy Red Pepper and Potato Soup...41

Creamy Broccoli and Potato Soup...43

Creamy Brussels Sprouts Soup..45

Creamy Potato Soup..47

Leek, Brown Rice and Potato Soup..49

Shredded Cabbage Soup..49

Carrot, Potato and Cabbage Soup..49

Cabbage, Tomato and Pasta Soup..49

Mediterranean Chickpea Soup...55

Carrot and Chickpea Soup..56

Carrot, Sweet Potato and Chickpea Soup.................................56

Sweet Potato and Coconut Soup...57

Creamy Tomato and Roasted Pepper Soup..............................58

Fresh Asparagus Soup..59

Creamy Red Lentil Soup...60

Lentil, Barley and Kale Soup..62

Mediterranean Lentil Soup..64

Curried Lentil and Parsnip Soup..66

Indian Chickpea Soup...68

Celery, Apple and Carrot Soup..72

Pea, Dill and Rice Soup..74

Minted Pea and Nettle Soup..75

Bean and Pasta Soup..77

Bean and Spinach Soup..79

Lima Bean Soup..81

Italian Minestrone..83

French Vegetable Soup..85

Spiced Beet and Carrot Soup..87

Pumpkin and Bell Pepper Soup...89

Mushroom Soup...90

Mushroom and Kale Soup..**90**

Spinach Soup...**92**

Nettle Soup..**93**

Brown Lentil Soup..**95**

Lemon Artichoke Soup...**95**

Creamy Artichoke Soup..**95**

Quinoa, Sweet Potato and Tomato Soup...............................**100**

Leek and Quinoa Soup..**102**

Red Lentil and Quinoa Soup..**104**

Spinach and Quinoa Soup...**106**

Vegetable Quinoa Soup...**108**

Tomato and Quinoa Soup...**110**

Kale, Leek and Quinoa Soup..**112**

FREE BONUS RECIPES: 20 Superfood Vegan Smoothies for Vibrant Health and Easy Weight Loss. .113

Superfood Soups To Boost Your Health

Soups are simply a miracle in a bowl for fat loss. They are quick to make, light and warming, but also nourishing, healing and soothing when prepared in the right way. Homemade superfood soups can really give you the figure of your dream and are a great meal, either as a healthy lunch, weeknight dinner or even for the festive season get-togethers. Superfood soups are the easiest filling food that can assist in your weight-loss efforts.

In my family we simply love soup and I prepare one every day. We even sometimes have soup for breakfast because soup only needs reheating and it is easily digestible yet nourishing. Prepared at home with simple vegetables and legumes, superfood soups are incredibly filling, crush carvings and will keep you energized for hours.

The superfood soups I am offering you in my new cookbook have been handed down from generation to generation over the years and I have personally tasted them all. Each recipe is packed with nourishing and nutrient-rich vegetables, herbs, whole grains, lean meats or beans. They have been slightly adapted to suit our modern tastes and are always absolutely delicious, healthy and budget friendly.

Creamy Chicken Soup

Serves: 4

Prep time: 35 min

Ingredients:

4 chicken breasts

1 carrot, chopped

1 cup zucchini, peeled and chopped

2 cups cauliflower, broken into florets

1 celery rib, chopped

1 small onion, chopped

5 cups water

1/2 tsp salt

black pepper, to taste

Directions:

Place chicken breasts, onion, carrot, celery, cauliflower and zucchini in a deep soup pot. Add in salt, black pepper and 5 cups of water. Stir and bring to a boil.

Simmer for 30 minutes then remove chicken from the pot and let it cool slightly.

Blend soup until completely smooth. Shred or dice the chicken meat, return it back to the pot, stir, and serve.

Thai Chicken and Mushroom Soup

Serves 4-5

Prep time: 10 min

Ingredients:

2 cups cooked and diced chicken

2 cups white button mushrooms

a bunch of spring onions

4 cups chicken broth

1 tbsp sugar

1 tbsp Thai red curry paste

1 tbsp Thai fish sauce

2 limes, juiced

salt and pepper, to taste

Directions:

In a deep soup pot, add broth, the curry paste, fish sauce, sugar and lime juice.

Bring to the boil, then add the mushrooms and whites of the green onions. Cover and simmer for 3-4 min.

Stir in the chicken and the spring onion greens. Cook for 2 minutes and serve with extra lime juice, sugar and fish sauce on the side.

Broccoli and Chicken Soup

Serves: 4

Prep time: 35 min

Ingredients:

4 boneless chicken thighs, diced

1 small carrot, chopped

1 broccoli head, broken into florets

1 garlic clove, chopped

1 small onion, chopped

4 cups water

3 tbsp extra virgin olive oil

1/2 tsp salt

black pepper, to taste

Directions:

In a deep soup pot, heat olive oil and gently sauté broccoli for 2-3 minutes, stirring occasionally. Add in onion, carrot, chicken and cook, stirring, for 2-3 minutes. Stir in salt, black pepper and water.

Bring to a boil. Simmer for 30 minutes then remove from heat and set aside to cool.

In a blender or food processor, blend soup until completely smooth. Serve and enjoy!

Warm Chicken and Avocado Soup

Serves 4

Prep time: 6-7 min

Ingredients:

2 ripe avocados, peeled and chopped

1 cooked chicken breast, shredded

1 garlic clove, chopped

3 cups chicken broth

salt and black pepper, to taste

fresh coriander leaves, finely cut, to serve

1/2 cup sour cream, to serve

Directions:

Combine avocados, garlic, and chicken broth in a blender. Process until smooth and transfer to a saucepan.

Add in chicken and cook, stirring, over medium heat until the mixture is hot. Serve topped with sour cream and finely cut coriander leaves.

Moroccan Chicken Soup

Serves: 5-6

Prep time: 30 min

Ingredients:

3-4 skinless, boneless chicken thighs, cut into bite-sized pieces

1 onion, finely cut

2 garlic cloves, chopped

1 small zucchini, peeled and diced

2 cups butternut squash, peeled and cut into bite-sized pieces

2 tbsp tomato paste

4 cups chicken broth

1/3 cup uncooked couscous

1/2 tsp ground cumin

1/4 tsp ground cinnamon

1 tbsp paprika

1 tsp dried basil

2 tsp orange zest

3 tbsp extra virgin olive oil

Directions:

Heat olive oil in a soup pot over medium heat. Gently sauté onion, for 1 minute, stirring. Add in garlic, basil and chicken, and cook for 2-3 minutes, or until chicken is sealed.

Stir in cumin, cinnamon and paprika. Add butternut squash and stir. Dissolve the tomato paste in the chicken broth and add to the soup.

Bring to a boil, reduce heat and simmer for 10-15 minutes.

Stir in couscous, salt, and zucchini and cook until the butternut squash is tender.

Remove from heat, season with salt and pepper to taste, stir in orange rind, and serve.

Spicy Chicken Quinoa Soup

Serves: 4-5

Prep time: 30 min

Ingredients:

2 chicken breast halves

2 carrots, chopped

1 celery stalk, chopped

1/2 onion, chopped

2 tomatoes, chopped

2 cups cooked quinoa

5 cups water

1 cup fresh or frozen peas

1 tsp cumin

1 tsp paprika

salt and black pepper, to taste

1/2 cup fresh coriander, finely cut, to serve

lemon juice, to serve

Directions:

Place chicken breasts in a soup pot together with onion, carrots, celery, peas, tomatoes, salt, black pepper, paprika, cumin, and water.

Bring to a boil, add in quinoa, stir, and reduce heat.

Simmer for 25 minutes then remove the chicken from the pot and let it cool slightly.

Shred the chicken and return it back to the pot. Stir, and serve sprinkled with fresh coriander and lemon juice.

Greek Lemon Chicken Soup

Serves: 4-5

Prep time: 35 min

Ingredients:

3 chicken breast halves, diced

1/3 cup rice

4 cups chicken broth

1 small onion, finely cut

3 raw egg yolks

1/2 cup fresh lemon juice

3 tbsp extra virgin olive oil

1 tsp salt

1/2 tsp black pepper

1/2 cup fresh parsley, finely cut, to serve

Directions:

In a soup pot, heat the olive oil and gently sauté the onion until translucent. Add in the chicken broth and bring to a boil.

Stir in the rice and the chicken, reduce heat, and simmer until the rice is almost done.

Whisk the egg yolks and lemon juice together in a small bowl. Gently add in a cup of the chicken soup whisking constantly. Return this mixture to the chicken soup and stir well to blend. Do not boil any more. Season with salt and pepper and garnish with finely chopped parsley. Serve hot.

Healthy Chicken and Oats Soup

Serves: 4-5

Prep time: 35 min

Ingredients:

3 chicken breasts, diced

1 small onion, chopped

3 garlic cloves

1/2 cup quick-cooking oats

1 large carrot, chopped

1 red bell pepper, chopped

1 celery rib, chopped

1 tomato, diced

5 cups water

1 bay leaf

1 tsp salt

1/2 cup fresh parsley leaves, finely cut

black pepper, to taste

Directions:

Place the chicken, bay leaf, celery, carrot, onion, red pepper, tomato and salt into a soup pot. Add in water and bring to the boil then reduce heat and simmer for 30 minutes.

Discard the bay leaf, season with salt and pepper, add in the oats and parsley, simmer for 5 more minutes, and serve.

Bean, Chicken and Bacon Soup

Serves 4-5

Prep time: 40 min

Ingredients:

2-3 bacon strips, chopped

2 cups cooked and diced chicken

1/2 can kidney beans, rinsed and drained

1 small onion, chopped

2 garlic cloves, chopped

3 cups water

1/2 can diced tomatoes, undrained

1 bay leaf

1/2 tsp dried oregano

1/2 tsp dried basil

salt and pepper, to taste

Directions:

In a deep soup pot, gently cook onion and bacon, stirring, for 3-4 minutes. Add in the garlic and cook until just fragrant.

Add in water, tomatoes and seasonings and bring to a boil. Cover, reduce heat and simmer for 30 minutes. Add in chicken and beans. Simmer for five minutes more and serve.

Asparagus and Chicken Soup

Serves 4

Prep time: 30 min

Ingredients:

2 chicken breast fillets, cooked and diced

2-3 leeks, finely cut

1 bunch asparagus, trimmed and cut

4 cups chicken broth

2 tbsp extra virgin olive oil

1/2 cup fresh parsley, finely chopped

salt and black pepper, to taste

lemon juice, to serve

Directions:

Heat the olive oil in a large soup pot. Add in the leeks and gently saute, stirring, for 2-3 minutes. Add chicken broth, the diced chicken, and bring to a boil. Reduce heat and simmer for 15 minutes.

Add in asparagus, parsley, salt and black pepper, and cook for 5 minutes more. Serve with lemon juice.

Italian Beef and Vegetable Soup

Serves: 4-5

Prep time: 40 min

Ingredients:

2 slices bacon, chopped

1 lb lean ground beef

1 carrot, chopped

2 cloves garlic, finely chopped

1 small onion, chopped

1 celery stalk, chopped

1 bay leaf

1 tsp dried basil

1 cup canned tomatoes, diced and drained

4 cups beef broth

1/2 cup canned chickpeas

½ cup vermicelli

Salt and black pepper, to taste

Directions:

In a large soup pot, cook bacon and ground beef until well done, breaking up the beef as it cooks. Drain off the fat and add in onion, garlic, carrot and celery. Cook for 3-4 minutes until fragrant. Stir in the bay leaf, basil, tomatoes and beef broth. Bring to a boil then reduce heat and simmer for about 20 minutes.

Add the chickpeas and vermicelli. Cook uncovered, for about 5 minutes more and serve.

Mediterranean Fish and Quinoa Soup

Serves: 4-5

Prep time: 30 min

Ingredients:

1 lb cod fillets, cubed

1 onion, chopped

3 tomatoes, chopped

1/2 cup quinoa, rinsed

1 red pepper, chopped

1 carrots, chopped

1/2 cup black olives, pitted and sliced

1 garlic clove, crushed

3 tbsp extra virgin olive oil

a pinch of cayenne pepper

1 bay leaf

1 tsp dried thyme

1 tsp dried dill

½ tsp pepper

½ cup white wine

4 cups water

salt and black pepper, to taste

1/2 cup fresh parsley, finely cut

Directions:

Heat the olive oil over medium heat and sauté the onion, red pepper, garlic and carrot until tender.

Stir in the cayenne pepper, bay leaf, herbs, salt and pepper. Add the white wine, water, quinoa and tomatoes and bring to a boil.

Reduce heat, cover, and cook for 10 minutes. Stir in olives and the fish and cook for another 10 minutes. Stir in parsley and serve hot.

Split Pea Soup with Ham and Barley

Serves: 4-5

Prep time: 35 min

Ingredients:

3/4 cup dry yellow split peas

2 carrots, chopped

1/2 lb low-sodium, nitrate-free, lean cooked ham, cut into 1/2-inch cubes

1 zucchini, peeled and diced

1 potato, peeled and diced

1 cup quick-cooking pearl barley

2 tsp dried sage

4 cups water

4 tbsp extra virgin olive oil

salt and black pepper, to taste

Directions:

In a medium pot, bring 2 cups water to a boil on high heat. Add split peas and reduce heat to medium-low. Simmer, uncovered, for 20 minutes. Drain and set aside.

Gently heat olive oil in a large soup pot. Add in onions, carrot and ham and cook for 1-2 minutes, stirring, until vegetables are tender.

Add in zucchini, sage, barley and water. Season to taste with salt and pepper and simmer for 15 minutes.

Alkalising Green Soup

Serves: 4-5

Prep time: 20 min

Ingredients:

2 cups broccoli, cut into florets and chopped

2 zucchinis, peeled and chopped

2 cups chopped kale

1 small onion, chopped

2-3 garlic cloves, chopped

4 cups vegetable broth

2 tbsp extra virgin olive oil

1/2 tsp ground ginger

1/2 tsp ground coriander

1 lime, juiced, to serve

Directions:

Gently heat olive oil in a large saucepan over medium-high heat. Cook onion and garlic for 3-4 minutes until tender. Add ginger and coriander and stir to coat well.

Add in broccoli, zucchinis, kale and vegetable broth. Bring to the boil, then reduce heat and simmer for 15 minutes, stirring from time to time.

Set aside to cool and blend until smooth. Return to pan and cook until heated through. Serve with lime juice.

Superfood Kale Soup

Serves: 4-5

Prep time: 20 min

Ingredients:

1 onion, chopped

2 carrots, chopped

2 cups chopped kale

2-3 garlic cloves, minced

4 cups vegetable broth

2 tbsp extra virgin olive oil

1/2 tsp ground ginger

1 tsp paprika

yogurt, to serve

Directions:

Gently heat olive oil in a large saucepan over medium-high heat. Cook onion, garlic and carrot for 3-4 minutes until tender. Add ginger and paprika and stir to coat well.

Add in kale and vegetable broth. Bring to the boil, then reduce heat and simmer for 15 minutes, stirring from time to time.

Set aside to cool and blend until smooth. Return to pan and cook until heated through. Serve with yogurt.

Cheesy Cauliflower Soup

Serves 4

Prep time: 5 min

Cooking time: 5-6 hours

Ingredients:

1 onion, chopped

1 head cauliflower, cut in florets

2 garlic cloves, minced

3 cups water

1 cup whole cream

1 cup cheddar cheese, grated

a pinch of thyme

salt, to taste

black pepper, to taste

Directions:

Put cauliflower, onion, garlic and water in the slow cooker. Cover and cook on low for 5-6 hours.

Blend in a blender, return to crockpot and stir in cream and cheese. Season with salt and pepper, stir to mix, and serve.

Slow Cooked Superfood Soup

Serves 4

Prep time: 5 min

Cooking time: 7 hours

Ingredients:

1 onion, chopped

2 garlic cloves, minced

2 carrots, chopped

1 turnip, diced

1 tomato, diced

1/4 cup dried lentils

2 cups chopped spinach

4 cups water

1/2 tsp dried basil

salt and black pepper, to taste

Directions:

Put all ingredients in the slow cooker. Cover and cook on high for 7 hours.

Turnip and Potato Soup

Serves 4-5

Prep time: 30 min

Ingredients:

1 onion, chopped

2 garlic cloves, minced

2 cups, diced potatoes

2 cups diced turnip

1 cup chopped kale

4 cups vegetable broth

1 cup heavy cream

3 tbsp extra virgin olive oil

1/2 tsp dried thyme

salt, to taste

black pepper, to taste

Directions:

Gently heat olive oil in a large saucepan over medium-high heat. Cook onion and garlic for 3-4 minutes until tender.

Add turnips, potatoes and the broth. Season with salt and black pepper to taste. Sprinkle with thyme and bring to a boil. Cover and simmer for 20 minutes or until the potato and turnip are tender.

Stir in the kale and the cream and allow to simmer together another 2-3 minutes.

Spicy Red Pepper and Potato Soup

Serves 4

Prep time: 30 min

Ingredients:

1 onion, chopped

2 garlic cloves, minced

2 carrots, chopped

2 red bell peppers, chopped

2 cups, diced potatoes

4 cups vegetable broth

3 tbsp extra virgin olive oil

1/2 tsp smoked paprika

1/4 tsp ginger

1/2 tsp dried sage

1/2 tsp cinnamon

1/2 tsp nutmeg

salt, to taste

black pepper, to taste

Directions:

Gently heat olive oil in a large saucepan over medium-high heat. Cook onion, garlic, carrot and the peppers together with all the spices for 3-4 minutes, stirring.

Add in potatoes and the broth. Season with salt and black pepper to taste. Cover and simmer for 20 minutes or until the potatoes and carrots are tender.

Creamy Broccoli and Potato Soup

Serves: 4-5

Prep time: 30 min

Ingredients:

3 cups broccoli, cut into florets and chopped

2 potatoes, peeled and chopped

1 large onion, chopped

3 garlic cloves, minced

1 cup raw cashews

1 cup vegetable broth

4 cups water

3 tbsp extra virgin olive oil

1/2 tsp ground nutmeg

Directions:

Soak cashews in a bowl covered with water for at least 4 hours. Drain water and blend cashews with 1 cup of vegetable broth until smooth. Set aside.

Gently heat olive oil in a large saucepan over medium-high heat. Cook onion and garlic for 3-4 minutes until tender. Add in broccoli, potato, nutmeg and water.

Cover and bring to the boil, then reduce heat and simmer for 20 minutes, stirring from time to time.

Remove from heat and stir in cashew mixture. Blend until smooth, return to pan and cook until heated through.

Creamy Brussels Sprouts Soup

Serves: 4-5

Prep time: 30 min

Ingredients:

1 lb frozen Brussels sprouts, thawed

2 potatoes, peeled and chopped

1 large onion, chopped

3 garlic cloves, minced

1 cup raw cashews

4 cups vegetable broth

3 tbsp extra virgin olive oil

1/2 tsp curry powder

salt and black pepper, to taste

Directions:

Soak cashews in a bowl covered with water for at least 4 hours. Drain water and blend cashews with 1 cup of vegetable broth until smooth. Set aside.

Gently heat olive oil in a large saucepan over medium-high heat. Cook onion and garlic and for 3-4 minutes until tender. Add in Brussels sprouts, potato, curry and vegetable broth.

Cover and bring to a boil, then reduce heat and simmer for 20 minutes, stirring from time to time. Remove from heat and stir in cashew mixture. Blend until smooth, return to pan and cook until heated through.

Creamy Potato Soup

Serves: 4-5

Prep time: 35 min

Ingredients:

5-6 medium potatoes, peeled and diced

1 leek, white part only, chopped

1 carrot, chopped

1 zucchini, peeled and chopped

1 celery stalk, chopped

3 cups water

1 cup coconut milk

3 tbsp extra virgin olive oil

salt and black pepper, to taste

Directions:

Gently heat olive oil in a deep saucepan and sauté the onion for 2-3 minutes. Add in potatoes, carrot, zucchini and celery and cook for 2-3 minutes, stirring.

Add in water and salt and bring to a boil, then lower heat and simmer until the vegetables are tender.

Blend until smooth, add coconut milk, blend some more and serve.

Leek, Brown Rice and Potato Soup

Serves: 4-5

Prep time: 35 min

Ingredients:

3 potatoes, peeled and diced

2 leeks, finely chopped

1/4 cup brown rice

5 cups water

3 tbsp extra virgin olive oil

lemon juice, to taste

Directions:

Heat olive oil in a deep soup pot and sauté leeks for 3-4 minutes.

Add in potatoes and cook for a minute more. Stir in water, bring to a boil, and the brown rice.

Reduce heat and simmer for 30 minutes. Add lemon juice, to taste, and serve.

Shredded Cabbage Soup

Serves: 4-5

Prep time: 30 min

Ingredients:

1 onion, chopped

1/2 head cabbage, shredded

1 carrot, chopped

1 potato, peeled and diced

1 celery stalk, sliced

1 can (15 oz) diced tomatoes, undrained

3 cups vegetable broth

1 tsp Italian seasoning

3 tbsp extra virgin olive oil

salt and pepper, to taste

Directions:

Heat the oil over medium heat and gently sauté the onion until translucent. Add in cabbage, carrot, potato, celery, tomatoes and seasoning and stir to combine.

Add in the broth, bring the soup to a boil, reduce heat, and simmer for 30-35 minutes. Season with salt and black pepper to taste.

Carrot, Potato and Cabbage Soup

Serves: 4-5

Prep time: 30 min

Ingredients:

1 onion, chopped

1/2 head red cabbage, shredded

2 carrots, chopped

2 potatoes, peeled and diced

4 cups chicken broth

1/2 tsp cumin

1 tsp paprika

4 tbsp extra virgin olive oil

salt and pepper, to taste

Directions:

In a deep saucepan, heat the oil over medium heat and gently sauté the onion until translucent. Add in the cabbage, carrots, potatoes, paprika and cumin and stir to coat well.

Add in the chicken broth and bring the soup to a boil, reduce heat, and simmer for 30-35 minutes. Season with salt and black pepper to taste.

Cabbage, Tomato and Pasta Soup

Serves: 4-5

Prep time: 30 min

Ingredients:

1 small onion, chopped

2 garlic cloves, chopped

1/2 head cabbage, shredded

1 carrot, chopped

3 large ripe tomatoes, diced

1/2 cup dried small pasta

4 cups chicken broth

1 tsp dried basil

1 tsp sugar

1 tbsp paprika

4 tbsp extra virgin olive oil

salt, to taste

black pepper, to taste

Directions:

In a deep saucepan, heat the oil over medium heat and gently sauté the onion and garlic until fragrant. Add in the cabbage, carrot, tomatoes, paprika, basil and sugar and stir to coat well.

Add in the chicken broth and bring the soup to a boil, reduce heat, and simmer for 10 minutes. Stir in the pasta and cook for 15 minutes more. Season with salt and black pepper to taste and serve.

Mediterranean Chickpea Soup

Serves 4-5

Ingredients:

1 can (15 oz) chickpeas, drained

1 small onion, chopped

2 garlic cloves, minced

1 can (15 oz) tomatoes, diced

2 cups water

2 cups coconut milk

3 tbsp extra virgin olive oil

2 bay leaves

1/2 tsp dried oregano

Directions:

Heat olive oil in a deep soup pot and sauté onion and garlic for 1-2 minutes. Add in water, chickpeas, tomatoes, bay leaves, and oregano.

Bring the soup to a boil then reduce heat and simmer for 20 minutes. Add in coconut milk and cook for 1-2 minutes more. Set aside to cool, discard the bay leaves and blend until smooth.

Carrot, Sweet Potato and Chickpea Soup

Serves: 5-6

Prep time: 25 min

Ingredients:

3 large carrots, chopped

1/2 onion, chopped

1 can (15 oz) chickpeas, undrained

2 sweet potatoes, peeled and diced

4 cups vegetable broth

2 tbsp extra virgin olive oil

1 tsp cumin

1 tsp ginger

Directions:

Heat olive oil in a large saucepan over medium heat. Add onion and carrots and sauté until tender.

Add in broth, chickpeas, sweet potato and seasonings. Bring to a boil then reduce heat and simmer, covered, for 30 minutes.

Blend soup until smooth, add coconut milk and cook for 2-3 minutes until heated through.

Sweet Potato and Coconut Soup

Serves: 4-5

Prep time: 25 min

Ingredients:

1 small onion, chopped

2 lb sweet potatoes, peeled and diced

4 cups vegetable broth

1 can coconut milk

2 tbsp extra virgin olive oil

1 tsp nutmeg

Directions:

Heat olive oil in a large saucepan over medium heat. Add onion and sauté until tender. Add in broth, sweet potato and nutmeg.

Bring to a boil then reduce heat and simmer, covered, for 30 minutes.

Blend soup until smooth and cook for 2-3 minutes until heated through.

Creamy Tomato and Roasted Pepper Soup

Serves: 4-5

Prep time: 35 min

Ingredients:

1 (12-ounce) jar roasted red peppers, drained and chopped

1 large onion, chopped

2 garlic cloves, minced

4 medium tomatoes, chopped

4 cups vegetable broth

3 tbsp extra virgin olive oil

2 bay leaves

Directions:

Heat olive oil in a large saucepan over medium-high heat and sauté onion for 3-4 minutes, stirring. Add in garlic and saute until just fragrant. Stir in the red peppers, bay leaves and tomatoes and simmer for 10 minutes.

Add broth, season with salt and pepper and bring to the boil. Reduce heat and simmer for 20 minutes.

Set aside to cool slightly, remove the bay leaves and blend, in batches, until smooth.

Fresh Asparagus Soup

Serves: 4-5

Prep time: 35 min

Ingredients:

2 lb fresh asparagus, cut into ½-inch pieces.

1 large onion, chopped

2 garlic cloves, minced

½ cup raw cashews, soaked in warm water for 1 hour

3 cups vegetable broth

3 tbsp extra virgin olive oil

lemon juice, to taste

Directions:

Heat olive oil in a large saucepan over medium-high heat and sauté onion for 3-4 minutes, stirring. Add in garlic and saute until just fragrant. Stir in asparagus and simmer for 5 minutes.

Add broth, season with salt and pepper and bring to the boil. Reduce heat and simmer for 20 minutes.

Set aside to cool slightly, add cashews, and blend, in batches, until smooth. Season with lemon juice and serve.

Creamy Red Lentil Soup

Serves: 4-5

Prep time: 35 min

Ingredients:

1 cup red lentils

1/2 small onion, chopped

2 garlic cloves, chopped

1/2 red pepper, chopped

3 cups vegetable broth

1 cup coconut milk

3 tbsp extra virgin olive oil

1 tbsp paprika

1/2 tsp ginger

1 tsp cumin

Directions:

Gently heat olive oil in a large saucepan. Add onion, garlic, red pepper, paprika, ginger and cumin and sauté, stirring, until just fragrant. Add in red lentils and vegetable broth.

Bring to a boil, cover, and simmer for 15 minutes. Add in coconut milk and simmer for 5 more minutes.

Remove from heat, season with salt and black pepper, and blend until smooth. Serve hot.

Lentil, Barley and Kale Soup

Serves: 4-5

Prep time: 35 min

Ingredients:

2 medium leeks, chopped

3 garlic cloves, chopped

2 bay leaves

1 can tomatoes (15 oz), diced and undrained

1/2 cup red lentils

1/2 cup barley

1 bunch kale (10 oz), stemmed and coarsely chopped

4 cups water

3 tbsp extra virgin olive oil

1 tsp paprika

½ tsp cumin

salt, to taste

black pepper, to taste

Directions:

Heat oil in a large saucepan over medium-high heat. Sauté leeks and garlic until just fragrant. Add cumin and paprika, tomatoes, lentils, barley, and water. Season with salt and pepper.

Cover and bring to the boil then reduce heat and simmer for 40 minutes or until barley is tender. Add in kale, stir it in, and let it simmer for five minutes more.

Mediterranean Lentil Soup

Serves: 4-5

Prep time: 20 min

Ingredients:

1 cup red lentils

2 carrots, chopped

1 onion, chopped

1 garlic clove, chopped

1 small red pepper, chopped

1 can tomatoes, chopped

½ can chickpeas, drained

½ can white beans, drained

1 celery stalk, chopped

6 cups water

1 tbsp paprika

1 tsp ginger, grated

1 tsp cumin

3 tbsp extra virgin olive oil

Directions:

Heat olive oil in a deep soup pot and gently sauté onions, garlic, red pepper and ginger. Add in water, lentils, chickpeas, white beans, tomatoes, carrots, celery, and cumin.

Bring to a boil then lower heat and simmer for 20 minutes, or until the lentils are tender. Purée half the soup in a food processor. Return the puréed soup to the pot, stir and serve.

Curried Lentil and Parsnip Soup

Serves: 4-5

Prep time: 35 min

Ingredients:

1 cup red lentils

5 medium parsnips, peeled and cut into chunks

1 onion, chopped

1 garlic clove, chopped

2 large apples, peeled, cored and cut into chunks

6 cups vegetable broth

3 tbsp curry paste

3 tbsp extra virgin olive oil

Directions:

1 cup Greek yogurt, to serve

Heat olive oil in a deep soup pot and gently sauté onions, garlic and curry paste. Add the parsnips, lentils and apple pieces.

Pour over the vegetable broth and bring to a simmer. Cook for 30 minutes, or until the parsnips are soft and the lentils mushy.

Remove from the heat and purée the soup in a food processor. Return the to the pot, and serve with yogurt.

Indian Chickpea Soup

Serves: 4-5

Prep time: 20 min

Ingredients:

2 carrots, chopped

1 small onion, chopped

1 cup green beans, chopped

1 garlic clove, minced

1 can chickpeas, undrained

4 cups vegetable broth

3-4 tbsp extra virgin olive oil

1 tbsp garam masala

1 tsp finely grated fresh root ginger

Directions:

Heat olive oil in a deep soup pot over medium-high heat. Gently sauté onion, garlic and carrots for 3-4 minutes, stirring. Add in ginger and gram masala and cook for 1 minute more, stirring.

Add vegetable broth and chickpeas. Bring to the boil then reduce heat and simmer, covered, for 15 minutes.

Blend soup until smooth and return to pan. Add in green beans and cook over medium-high heat for 3-5 minutes.

Season with salt and pepper to taste, and serve with naan bread.

Carrot and Chickpea Soup

Serves: 4-5

Prep time: 20 min

Ingredients:

4 carrots, chopped

1 onion, chopped

1 garlic clove, minced

1 can chickpeas, undrained

4 cups vegetable broth

3-4 tbsp extra virgin olive oil

1 tsp paprika

1 tsp grated ginger

salt and black pepper, to taste

Directions:

Heat olive oil in a deep soup pot over medium-high heat. Gently sauté onion, garlic and carrots for 3-4 minutes, stirring. Add in paprika, ginger, broth and chickpeas.

Bring to the boil then reduce heat and simmer, covered, for 10 minutes.

Blend the soup until smooth and return to pan. Cook over medium-high heat until heated through. Season with salt and pepper to taste and serve.

Celery, Apple and Carrot Soup

Serves: 4-5

Prep time: 20 min

Ingredients:

2 celery stalks, chopped

1 large apple, chopped

1/2 onion, chopped

2 carrots, chopped

1 garlic clove, minced

4 cups vegetable broth

3-4 tbsp extra virgin olive oil

1 tsp paprika

1 tsp grated ginger

salt and black pepper, to taste

Directions:

Heat olive oil in a deep soup pot over medium-high heat. Gently sauté onion, garlic and carrots for 3-4 minutes, stirring. Add in paprika, ginger, celery, apple and broth.

Bring to the boil then reduce heat and simmer, covered, for 10 minutes.

Blend soup until smooth and return to pan. Cook over medium-high heat until heated through. Season with salt and pepper to taste and serve.

Pea, Dill and Rice Soup

Serves: 4

Prep time: 10 min

Ingredients:

1 (16 oz) bag frozen green peas

1 onion, chopped

3-4 garlic cloves, chopped

1/3 cup rice

3 tbsp fresh dill, chopped

3 tbsp extra virgin olive oil

fresh dill, finely chopped, to serve

salt and pepper, to taste

Directions:

Heat oil in a large saucepan over medium-high heat and sauté onion and garlic for 3-4 minutes.

Add in peas and vegetable broth and bring to the boil. Stir in rice, cover, reduce heat, and simmer for 15 minutes. Add dill, season with salt and pepper and serve sprinkled with fresh dill.

Minted Pea and Nettle Soup

Serves: 4

Prep time: 10 min

Ingredients:

1 onion, chopped

3-4 garlic cloves, chopped

4 cups vegetable broth

2 tbsp dried mint leaves

1 16 oz bag frozen green peas

about 20 nettle tops

3 tbsp extra virgin olive oil

fresh dill, finely chopped, to serve

Directions:

Heat oil in a large saucepan over medium-high heat and sauté onion and garlic for 3-4 minutes.

Add in dried mint, peas, washed nettles, and vegetable broth and bring to the boil.

Cover, reduce heat, and simmer for 10 minutes. Remove from heat and set aside to cool slightly, then blend in batches, until smooth. Return soup to saucepan over medium-low heat and cook until heated through. Season with salt and pepper. Serve sprinkled with fresh dill.

Bean and Pasta Soup

Serves: 4-5

Prep time: 10-15 min

Ingredients:

1 onion, chopped

2 large carrots, chopped

2 garlic cloves, minced

1 cup cooked orzo

1 15 oz can white beans, rinsed and drained

1 15 oz can tomatoes, diced and undrained

1 cup baby spinach leaves

3 cups water

1 tbsp paprika

1 tbsp dried mint

3 tbsp extra virgin olive oil

salt, to taste

black pepper, to taste

Directions:

Heat the olive oil over medium heat and gently sauté the onion, garlic and carrots. Add in tomatoes, water, salt and pepper, and bring to a boil.

Reduce heat and cook for 5-10 minutes, or until the carrots are tender. Stir in orzo, beans and spinach, and simmer until spinach is wilted.

Bean and Spinach Soup

Serves: 4-5

Prep time: 10-15 min

Ingredients:

1 onion, chopped

1 large carrot, chopped

2 garlic cloves, minced

1 15 oz can white beans, rinsed and drained

1 cup spinach leaves, trimmed and washed

3 cups vegetable broth

1 tbsp paprika

1 tbsp dried mint

3 tbsp extra virgin olive oil

salt and black pepper, to taste

Directions:

Heat the olive oil over medium heat and gently sauté the onion, garlic and carrot. Add in beans, broth, salt and pepper and bring to a boil. Reduce heat and cook for 10 minutes, or until the carrots are tender.

Stir in spinach, and simmer for about 5 minutes, until spinach is wilted.

Lima Bean Soup

Serves: 5-6

Prep time: 3-4 hrs for soaking, 120 min for cooking

Ingredients:

1 lb dry lima beans

4-5 cups water

2 leeks, white part only, chopped

1 small onion, finely cut

1 celery stalk, chopped

3 carrots, chopped

5 cups vegetable broth

4 tbsp extra virgin olive oil

salt and black pepper, to taste

Directions:

Wash the lima beans and soak them in water for a few hours. Discard the water, pour 3 cups of fresh water and cook the beans for an hour; discard this water too.

In a deep soup pot, heat olive oil and sauté the onion, leeks, celery and carrots until tender-crisp. Add 5 cups of vegetable broth and the lima beans. Stir, bring to the boil, lower heat and simmer for 1 hour.

Season with salt and black pepper and purée half the soup in a food processor. Return the puréed soup to the pot, stir and serve.

Italian Minestrone

Serves: 4-5

Prep time: 25 min

Ingredients:

1/2 onion, chopped

2 garlic cloves, chopped

¼ cabbage, chopped

1 carrot, chopped

2 celery stalks, chopped

3 cups water

1 cup canned tomatoes, diced, undrained

1 1/2 cup green beans, trimmed and cut into 1/2-inch pieces

1/2 cup pasta, cooked

2-3 fresh basil leaves

2 tbsp extra virgin olive oil

black pepper, to taste

salt, to taste

Directions:

Heat the olive oil in a large pot over medium-high heat. Add the onion and cook until translucent, about 4 minutes. Add in the garlic, carrot and celery and cook for 5 minutes more.

Stir in the green beans, cabbage, tomatoes, basil, and water and bring to a boil.

Reduce heat and simmer uncovered, for 15 minutes, or until vegetables are tender.

Stir in the pasta, season with pepper and salt to taste and serve.

French Vegetable Soup

Serves: 4-5

Prep time: 25 min

Ingredients:

2 leeks, white and pale green parts only, well rinsed and thinly sliced

1 large zucchini, peeled and diced

1 medium fennel bulb, trimmed, cored, and cut into large chunks

2 garlic cloves, chopped

3 cups vegetable broth

1 cup canned tomatoes, drained and chopped

1/2 cup vermicelli, broken into small pieces

3 tbsp extra virgin olive oil

black pepper, to taste

Directions:

Heat the olive oil in a large stockpot. Add the leeks and saute over low heat for 5 minutes. Add in the zucchini, fennel and garlic and cook for about 5 minutes.

Stir in the vegetable broth and the tomatoes and bring to the boil. Reduce heat and simmer, uncovered, for 20 minutes, or until the vegetables are tender but still holding their shape. Stir in the vermicelli. Simmer for a further 5 minutes and serve.

Spiced Beet and Carrot Soup

Serves: 4-5

Prep time: 25 min

Ingredients:

3 beets, washed and peeled

2 carrots, peeled and chopped

1 small onion, chopped

1 garlic clove, chopped

3 cups vegetable broth

1 cup water

2 tbsp extra virgin olive oil

1 tsp grated ginger

1 tsp grated orange peel

Directions:

Heat the olive oil in a large stockpot. Add the onion and saute over low heat for 3-4 minutes or until translucent.

Add the garlic, beets, carrots, ginger and lemon rind. Stir in water and vegetable broth and bring to the boil.

Reduce heat to medium and simmer, partially covered, for 30 minutes, or until the beets are tender. Cool slightly and blend soup in batches until smooth. Season with salt and pepper and serve.

Pumpkin and Bell Pepper Soup

Serves: 4-5

Prep time: 35 min

Ingredients:

1/2 small onion, chopped

3 cups pumpkin cubes

2 red bell peppers, chopped

1 carrot, chopped

3 cups vegetable broth

3 tbsp extra virgin olive oil

1/2 tsp cumin

salt and black pepper, to taste

Directions:

Heat the olive oil in a deep soup pot and sauté the onion for 4-5 minutes. Add in the pumpkin, carrot and bell peppers and cook, stirring, for 5 minutes. Stir in broth and cumin and bring to the boil.

Reduce heat to low, cover, and simmer, stirring occasionally, for 30 minutes, or until vegetables are soft. Season with salt and pepper, blend in batches and reheat to serve.

Mushroom Soup

Serves: 4-5

Prep time: 35 min

Ingredients:

2 lbs mushrooms, peeled and chopped

1 large onion, chopped

2 garlic cloves, minced

3 cups vegetable broth

salt and pepper, to taste

3 tbsp extra virgin olive oil

Directions:

Sauté onions and garlic in a large soup pot untill transparent. Add thyme and mushrooms.

Stir and cook for 10 minutes, then add the vegetable broth and simmer for another 10-20 minutes. Blend, season and serve.

Mushroom and Kale Soup

Serves: 4-5

Prep time: 30 min

Ingredients:

1 onion, chopped

1 carrot, chopped

1 zucchini, peeled and diced

1 potato, peeled and diced

10 white mushrooms, chopped

1 bunch kale (10 oz), stemmed and coarsely chopped

3 cups vegetable broth

4 tbsp extra virgin olive oil

salt and black pepper. to taste

Directions:

Gently heat olive oil in a large soup pot. Add in onions, carrot and mushrooms and cook until vegetables are tender.

Stir in the zucchini, kale and vegetable broth. Season to taste with salt and pepper and simmer for 20 minutes.

Spinach Soup

Serves: 4-5

Prep time: 35 min

Ingredients:

14 oz frozen spinach, slightly thawed

1 large onion, chopped

1 small carrot, chopped

1 small zucchini, peeled and chopped

3 cups hot water

4 tbsp extra virgin olive oil

1 tbsp paprika

salt and black pepper, to taste

salt, to taste

Directions:

Heat oil in a deep cooking pot. Add in the onion and carrot and cook for 3-4 minutes, until tender. Add in paprika, spinach, zucchini and water and stir. Season with salt and black pepper and bring to the boil.

Reduce heat and simmer for around 30 minutes.

Nettle Soup

Serves 6-7

Prep time: 20 min

Ingredients:

2 lbs young top shoots of nettles, well washed

2 potatoes, diced small

5-6 spring onions, chopped

3 cups water

1 cup soy milk

3-4 tbsp extra virgin olive oil

1 tsp salt

3 tbsp chopped fresh mint

Directions:

Clean the nettles, wash and cook them in slightly salted water for 1-2 minutes.

Discard the water and chop the nettles finely.

In a soup pot, gently sauté the spring onions and potatoes in olive oil for 2-3 minutes, stirring. Add in the nettles and 3 cups of water. Stir well, then simmer until the potatoes are cooked through.

Add soy milk, blend until smooth, sprinkle with mint and serve.

Brown Lentil Soup

Serves: 4-5

Prep time: 35 min

Ingredients:

1 cup brown lentils

1 small onion, chopped

4 garlic cloves, minced

1 medium carrot, chopped

1 medium tomato, diced

3 cups warm water

4 tbsp extra virgin olive oil

1 tbsp paprika

1 tbsp summer savory

Directions:

Heat olive oil in a deep soup pot and cook the onions and carrots until tender. Add in paprika, garlic, lentils, savory and water, stir, and bring to the boil.

Reduce heat and cook, covered, for 30 minutes. Add tomato and salt and simmer for 10 minutes more.

Lemon Artichoke Soup

Serves: 4-5

Prep time: 35 min

Ingredients:

3 cups artichoke hearts, chopped

1/2 onion, chopped

1 celery stalk, chopped

1 carrot, chopped

2 garlic cloves, minced

2 cups vegetable broth

2 tbsp olive oil

1 tsp salt

2 tbsp lemon juice

1 cup coconut milk

Directions:

Heat olive oil in a large pot and gently sauté the onion, celery, carrot, and garlic until the onion and garlic are translucent. Stir in vegetable broth, artichokes and salt and bring to the boil.

Reduce heat, add lemon juice and simmer for 15 minutes. Set aside to cool and blend until smooth. Stir in the coconut milk and simmer for another 5 minutes.

Creamy Artichoke Soup

Serves: 4-5

Prep time: 35 min

Ingredients:

3 cups artichoke hearts, chopped

1/2 onion, chopped

2 celery stalk, chopped

1 small potato, peeled and chopped

2 garlic cloves, minced

2 cups vegetable broth

1 cup coconut milk

2 tbsp olive oil

1 tsp salt

black pepper, to serve

Directions:

Heat olive oil in a large pot and gently sauté the onion, celery and garlic until just fragrant. Stir in the vegetable broth, coconut milk, artichokes and salt and bring to the boil.

Reduce heat and simmer for 15 minutes. Set aside to cool and blend until smooth. Serve sprinkled with black pepper.

Quinoa, Sweet Potato and Tomato Soup

Serves: 4

Prep time: 20 min

Ingredients:

½ cup quinoa

1 onion, chopped

1 large sweet potato, peeled and chopped

½ cup canned chickpeas, drained

1 cup baby spinach leaves

1 can tomatoes, drained and diced

3 cups vegetable broth

1 cup water

2 cloves garlic, chopped

1 tbsp grated fresh ginger

1 tsp cumin

1 tbsp paprika

2 tbsp extra virgin olive oil

Directions:

Wash quinoa very well, drain and set aside.

In a large soup pot, heat the olive oil over medium heat. Add the onions and garlic and sauté about 1-2 minutes, stirring. Add the sweet potato and sauté for another minute then add in the paprika, ginger and cumin. Add water and broth, bring to a boil and stir in quinoa and tomatoes.

Reduce heat to low, cover, and simmer about 15 minutes, or until the sweet potatoes are tender. Season with salt and black pepper to taste. Blend the soup and return to the pot. Add the chickpeas and heat through, then add the spinach and cook until it wilts.

Leek and Quinoa Soup

Serves: 4-5

Prep time: 15 min

Ingredients:

½ cup quinoa

3 leeks, white part only, sliced

3 garlic cloves, chopped

1 potato, cut in small cubes

½ cup canned chickpeas, drained

4 cups vegetable broth

1 cup coconut milk

2 tbsp extra virgin olive oil

½ tsp ground coriander

1 tsp turmeric

salt and black pepper, to taste

Directions:

In a large soup pot, heat the olive oil over medium heat. Add the garlic and sauté for 1-2 minutes, stirring. Add the spices and stir. Add the broth and bring to the boil then add in the quinoa, leeks, chickpeas and potato.

Reduce heat and simmer, covered, for 15 minutes. When the leeks are soft, add in a cup of coconut milk, stir, and simmer for 2 more minutes.

Red Lentil and Quinoa Soup

Serves: 4

Prep time: 20 min

Ingredients:

½ cup quinoa

1 cup red lentils

5 cups water

1 onion, chopped

2-3 garlic cloves, chopped

½ red bell pepper, finely cut

1 small tomato, chopped

3 tbsp extra virgin olive oil

1 tsp ginger

1 tsp cummin

1 tbsp paprika

salt, to taste

black pepper, to taste

Directions:

Wash and drain quinoa and red lentils and set aside.

In a large soup pot, heat the olive oil over medium heat. Add the onion, garlic and red pepper and sauté for 1-2 minutes, stirring. Add the paprika and spices and stir. Add in the red lentils and quinoa, stir and add the water.

Gently bring to the boil, then lower heat and simmer, covered for 15 minutes. Add the tomato and cook for five more minutes. Blend the soup, serve and enjoy!

Spinach and Quinoa Soup

Serves: 4-5

Prep time: 20 min

Ingredients:

½ cup quinoa

1 onion, chopped

1 garlic clove, chopped

1 small zucchini, peeled and diced

1 tomato, diced

2 cups fresh spinach, cut

4 cups water

3 tbsp extra virgin olive oil

1 tbsp paprika

salt and pepper, to taste

Directions:

Heat olive oil in a deep soup pot over medium-high heat. Add onion and garlic and sauté for 1 minute, stirring constantly. Add in paprika and the zucchini, stir, and cook for 2-3 minutes more.

Add 4 cups of water and bring to a boil then add in spinach and quinoa. Stir and reduce heat. Simmer for 15 minutes then set aside to cool.

Vegetable Quinoa Soup

Serves: 4-5

Prep time: 20 min

Ingredients:

½ cup quinoa

1 cup sliced leeks

1 garlic clove, chopped

½ carrot, diced

1 tomato, diced

1 small zucchini, diced

½ cup frozen green beans

4 cups water

1 tsp paprika

4 tbsp extra virgin olive oil

5-6 tbsp lemon juice, to serve

Directions:

Wash quinoa in a fine sieve under running water until the water runs clear. Set aside to drain.

Heat olive oil in a soup pot and gently sauté the leeks, garlic and carrot for 1 minute, stirring. Add paprika, the zucchini, tomatoes, green beans and water.

Bring to a boil, add quinoa and lower heat to medium-low. Simmer for 15 minutes, or until the vegetables are tender. Serve with lemon juice.

Tomato and Quinoa Soup

Serves: 4-5

Prep time: 35 min

Ingredients:

4 cups chopped fresh tomatoes

1 onion, chopped

1/3 cup quinoa

2 cups water

1 garlic clove, minced

3 tbsp extra virgin olive oil

1 tbsp paprika

1 tsp salt

½ tsp black pepper

1 tbsp sugar

fresh parsley, chopped, to serve

Directions:

Heat olive oil in a large soup pot and saute onions until translucent. Add in paprika, garlic and tomatoes and water and bring to the boil.

Simmer for 10 minutes then blend the soup and return it to the pot. Add the very well washed quinoa and a tablespoon of sugar and bring to the boil again. Simmer for 15 minutes stirring occasionally. Serve sprinkled with parsley.

Kale, Leek and Quinoa Soup

Serves: 4-5

Prep time: 35 min

Ingredients:

½ cup quinoa

2 leeks, white part only, chopped

1/2 onion, chopped

1 can tomatoes, diced and undrained

1 bunch kale (10 oz), stemmed and coarsely chopped

4 cups vegetable broth

3 tbsp extra virgin olive oil

salt and pepper, to taste

Directions:

Heat olive oil in a large pot over medium heat and gently sauté the onion for 3-4 minutes. Add in the leeks, season with salt and pepper and add the vegetable broth, tomatoes and quinoa.

Bring to a boil then reduce heat and simmer for 10 minutes. Stir in the kale and cook for another 5 minutes.

Free Bonus Recipes: 20 Superfood Vegan Smoothies for Vibrant Health and Easy Weight Loss

Kale and Kiwi Smoothie

Serves: 2

Prep time: 2-3 min

Ingredients:

2-3 ice cubes

1 cup orange juice

1 small pear, peeled and chopped

2 kiwi, peeled and chopped

2-3 kale leaves

2-3 dates, pitted

Directions:

Combine all ingredients in a high speed blender and blend until smooth.

Delicious Broccoli Smoothie

Serves: 2

Prep time: 2-3 min

Ingredients:

2-3 frozen broccoli florets

1 cup coconut milk

1 banana, peeled and chopped

1 cup pineapple, cut

1 peach, chopped

1 tsp cinnamon

Directions:

Combine all ingredients in a high speed blender and blend until smooth.

Papaya Smoothie

Serves: 2

Prep time: 2-3 min

Ingredients:

2-3 frozen broccoli florets

1 cup orange juice

1 small ripe avocado, peeled, cored and diced

1 cup papaya

1 cup fresh strawberries

Directions:

Combine all ingredients in a high speed blender and blend until smooth.

Beet and Papaya Smoothie

Serves: 2

Prep time: 2-3 min

Ingredients:

3-4 ice cubes

1 cup orange juice

1 banana, peeled and chopped

1 cup papaya

1 small beet, peeled and cut

Directions:

Combine all ingredients in a high speed blender and blend until smooth.

Lean Green Smoothie

Serves: 2

Prep time: 2-3 min

Ingredients:

1 frozen banana, chopped

1 cup orange juice

2-3 kale leaves, stems removed

1 small cucumber, peeled and chopped

1/2 cup fresh parsley leaves

½ tsp grated ginger

Directions:

Combine all ingredients in a high speed blender and blend until smooth.

Easy Antioxidant Smoothie

Serves: 2

Prep time: 2-3 min

Ingredients:

2-3 frozen broccoli florets

1 cup orange juice

2 plums, cut

1 cup raspberries

1 tsp ginger powder

Directions:

Combine all ingredients in a high speed blender and blend until smooth.

Healthy Purple Smoothie

Serves: 2

Prep time: 2-3 min

Ingredients:

2-3 frozen broccoli florets

1 cup water

1/2 avocado, peeled and chopped

3 plums, chopped

1 cup blueberries

Directions:

Combine all ingredients in a high speed blender and blend until smooth.

Mom's Favorite Kale Smoothie

Serves: 2

Prep time: 2-3 min

Ingredients:

2-3 ice cubes

1½ cup orange juice

1 green small apple, cut

½ cucumber, chopped

2-3 leaves kale

½ cup raspberries

Directions:

Combine all ingredients in a high speed blender and blend until smooth.

Creamy Green Smoothie

Serves: 2

Prep time: 2-3 min

Ingredients:

1 frozen banana

1 cup coconut milk

1 small pear, chopped

1 cup baby spinach

1 cup grapes

1 tbsp coconut butter

1 tsp vanilla extract

Directions:

Combine all ingredients in a high speed blender and blend until smooth.

Strawberry and Arugula Smoothie

Serves: 2

Prep time: 2-3 min

Ingredients:

2 cups frozen strawberries

1 cup unsweetened almond milk

10-12 arugula leaves

1/2 tsp ground cinnamon

Directions:

Combine ice, almond milk, strawberries, arugula and cinnamon in a high speed blender. Blend until smooth and serve.

Emma's Amazing Smoothie

Serves: 2

Prep time: 2-3 min

Ingredients:

1 frozen banana, chopped

1 cup orange juice

1 large nectarine, sliced

1/2 zucchini, peeled and chopped

2-3 dates, pitted

Directions:

Combine all ingredients in a high speed blender and blend until smooth.

Good-To-Go Morning Smoothie

Serves: 2

Prep time: 2-3 min

Ingredients:

1 cup frozen strawberries

1 cup apple juice

1 banana, chopped

1 cup raw asparagus, chopped

1 tbsp ground flaxseed

Directions:

Combine all ingredients in a high speed blender and blend until smooth.

Endless Energy Smoothie

Serves: 2

Prep time: 2-3 min

Ingredients:

1 frozen banana, chopped

1 1/2 cup green tea

1 cup chopped pineapple

2 raw asparagus spears, chopped

1 lime, juiced

1 tbsp chia seeds

Directions:

Combine all ingredients in a high speed blender and blend until smooth.

High-fibre Fruit Smoothie

Serves: 2

Prep time: 2-3 min

Ingredients:

1 frozen banana, chopped

1 cup orange juice

2 cups chopped papaya

1 cup shredded cabbage

1 tbsp chia seeds

Directions:

Combine all ingredients in a high speed blender and blend until smooth.

Nutritious Green Smoothie

Serves: 2

Prep time: 2-3 min

Ingredients:

2-3 frozen broccoli florets

1 cup apple juice

1 large pear, chopped

1 kiwi, peeled and chopped

1 cup spinach leaves

1-2 dates, pitted

Directions:

Combine all ingredients in a high speed blender and blend until smooth.

Apricot, Strawberry and Banana Smoothie

Serves: 2

Prep time: 2-3 min

Ingredients:

1 frozen banana

1 1/2 cup almond milk

5 dried apricots

1 cup fresh strawberries

Directions:

Combine all ingredients in a high speed blender and blend until smooth.

Spinach and Green Apple Smoothie

Serves: 2

Prep time: 2-3 min

Ingredients:

3-4 ice cubes

1 cup unsweetened almond milk

1 banana, peeled and chopped

2 green apples, peeled and chopped

1 cup raw spinach leaves

3-4 dates, pitted

1 tsp grated ginger

Directions:

Combine all ingredients in a high speed blender and blend until smooth.

Superfood Blueberry Smoothie

Serves: 2

Prep time: 2-3 min

Ingredients:

2-3 cubes frozen spinach

1 cup green tea

1 banana

2 cups blueberries

1 tbsp ground flaxseed

Directions:

Combine all ingredients in a high speed blender and blend until smooth.

Zucchini and Blueberry Smoothie

Serves: 2

Prep time: 2-3 min

Ingredients:

1 cup frozen blueberries

1 cup unsweetened almond milk

1 banana

1 zucchini, peeled and chopped

Directions:

Combine all ingredients in a high speed blender and blend until smooth.

Tropical Spinach Smoothie

Serves: 2

Prep time: 2-3 min

Ingredients:

1/2 cup crushed ice or 3-4 ice cubes

1 cup coconut milk

1 mango, peeled and diced

1 cup fresh spinach leaves

4-5 dates, pitted

1/2 tsp vanilla extract

Directions:

Combine all ingredients in a high speed blender and blend until smooth.

About the Author

Alissa Grey lives in a small French village in the foothills of a beautiful mountain range with her husband, three teenage kids, two free spirited dogs, and various other animals.

She is incredibly lucky to be able to cook and eat natural foods, mostly grown nearby, something she's done since she was a teenager. Alissa enjoys reading, hanging out with her family, going for long hikes, and growing organic vegetables and herbs.